HISTORY & GEOGRAPHY 303
A FRUIT-GROWING COMMUNITY
IN WASHINGTON

CONTENTS

Author: **Mary Vandermey**

Editor-In-Chief: Richard W. Wheeler, M.A.Ed.

Editor: Martha K. Baxter, M.A.Ed.

Consulting Editor: Howard Stitt, TH.M., Ed.D.

Revision Editor: Alan Christopherson, M.S.

Alpha Omega Publications®

804 N. 2nd Ave. E., Rock Rapids, IA 51246-1759

Learn with our friends:

When you see me, I will help your teacher explain the exciting things you are expected to do.

When you do actions with me, you will learn how to write, draw, match words, read, and much more.

You and I will learn about matching words, listening, drawing, and other fun things in your lessons.

A FRUIT-GROWING COMMUNITY IN WASHINGTON

You will read in this LIFEPAC® about apple growing that is a community project. Many people who know how to do many different tasks work together to bring apples to you.

After finishing this study, you may want to visit the state of Washington.

You will want to see the great mountains, rivers, and lakes. You will want to see Grand Coulee Dam, one of the largest concrete dams in the world.

 **Objectives**

Read these objectives. They tell you what you will be able to do when you have finished this LIFEPAC.

1. You will be able to find the state of Washington on the map.
2. You will be able to tell what states, country, and ocean are next to Washington.
3. You will be able to tell about the geography of Washington.
4. You will be able to tell how apple growers care for their trees in winter and in spring.

1 (one)

5. You will be able to tell how many people, doing different things, help to bring apples to you.
6. You will be able to tell how bees help the growers.
7. You will be able to name different kinds of apples.
8. You will be able to tell how Christian people help each other.

NEW WORDS

acre (a cre). A measure of land.

bandage (band age). Strip of cloth used to wrap a wound.

bin. Large box for holding things.

border (bor der). The side, edge, or part near anything.

breathe. Draw air in and out.

bruise. Mark on the outside of a fruit caused by poor handling.

canvas (can vas). A strong cloth.

capital (cap i tal). Most important or leading place.

cluster (clus ter). A number of things of the same kind growing together.

codling moth (cod ling moth). A small insect that can harm apples.

conveyor (con vey or). A moving belt that carries things from one place to another.

dairy (dair y). Farm where milk is produced.

eastern (east ern). Toward the east.

elevation (el e va tion). How high a place is above sea level.

festival (fes ti val). A special day to honor some great thing that has happened.

freckles (freck les). Small, light-brown spots on the skin.

grade. Place in order of how good or bad something is.

harvest (har vest). The time when crops are brought in.

heal. Make well.

irrigate (ir ri gate). Get water to the land by using ditches.

juicy (juic y). Runny, full of juice.

lopsided (lop sid ed). Larger on one side than on the other.

nectar (nec tar). Sweet liquid found in flowers.

nursery (nurs er y). Place where young trees or plants are raised for sale.

orchard (or chard). Piece of ground on which fruit trees are grown.

polisher (pol ish er). Something or someone who makes something smooth and shiny.

pollen (pol len). A fine, yellow dust found inside flowers.

prop. Hold up by placing something under or against.

prune. Cut out branches that are not wanted.

rotten (rot ten). Spoiled.

spillway (spill way). Place for water to escape when a dam gets too full.

temperature (tem per a ture). How hot or cold something is.

thorn. Sharp-pointed part on the stem or branch of a tree or plant.

tray. A flat holder with a rim around it.

welcome (wel come). To give a friendly greeting.

western (west ern). Toward the west.

These words will appear in **boldface** (darker print) the first time they are used.

I. A NEW HOME IN WASHINGTON

You will travel with Debra and Joe Sanders to their new home in Washington, in this section of your LIFEPAC. You will learn a few funny ways you talk about apples. You will see how Christian people help each other. You will learn about the care of apple trees in winter.

border	(bor der)	The side, edge, or part near anything.
eastern	(east ern)	Toward the east.
orchard	(or chard)	Piece of ground on which fruit trees are grown.
polisher	(pol ish er)	Something or someone who makes something smooth and shiny.
rotten	(rot ten)	Spoiled.
welcome	(wel come)	To give a friendly greeting.
western	(west ern)	Toward the west.

SPECIAL WORDS

Cascade Mountains   Tacoma
Columbia River   Walla Walla
Mount Rainier   Washington
Oregon   Wenatchee
Pacific Ocean

 Ask your teacher to say these words with you.
Teacher check _____
                          Initial   Date

SAYINGS ABOUT APPLES

Joe and Debra Sanders looked out of the window of the car. They saw their new home state for the first time.

Their father said, "That river we just crossed is the Columbia River. It has lots of good fishing. We are now in Washington. It won't be long until we see the **orchards** of my old home where we will live. I'm glad we are coming now. You can see what the apple trees look like in winter."

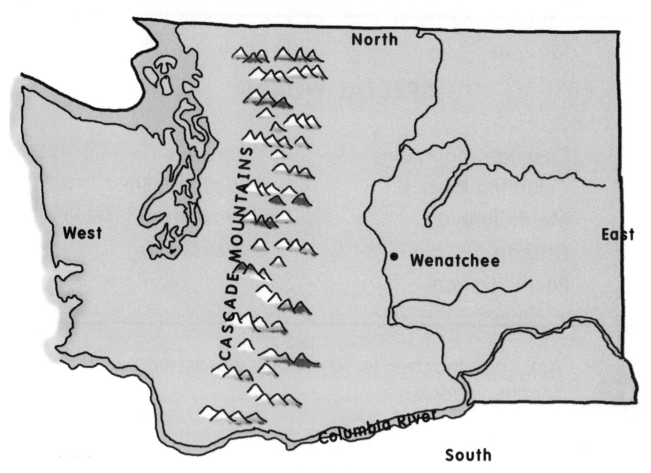

North

West

CASCADE MOUNTAINS

Wenatchee

East

Columbia River

South

Washington

Mrs. Sanders said, "While we are waiting, let's think of some 'apple sayings.'"

"I know one," Debra said. "'The apple of your eye' means you think a lot of the person you're talking about."

Joe came next. "'An apple a day keeps the doctor away' means apples are good for you. They give you pep."

Debra was ready again. "If you say someone is a '**rotten** apple,' that means a person is bad. But I think God doesn't like to have us say people are bad. We ought to look for the good in a person."

It was Joe's turn. "If you are 'an apple **polisher**', you're trying to get someone to be extra nice to you."

Mrs. Sanders said, "If I say, 'Applesauce!', what does that mean?"

Debra said, "You think what someone has said is silly!"

Mr. Sanders had his turn. "'You upset my apple cart' means you spoiled a plan I had."

Mrs. Sanders had another one. "I try to keep the house in 'apple-pie order', but some children I know leave their jackets and books scattered about!"

Everybody laughed. Joe and Debra hid their faces behind their hands.

Do this activity.

1.1   Write down three of the "apple sayings" you remember reading about here. Can you think of other sayings about apples? Write any sayings you think of on the lines.

_____

_____

_____

_____

_____

_____

GEOGRAPHY OF WASHINGTON

"Look, everybody! See the Cascade Mountains! They divide Washington in half," said Father.

There they were! The mountains seemed to reach to the sky. Many mountains were snow-capped. Mr. Sanders told them how useful those mountains were to apple growers.

"The mountains shut off heavy rains coming in from the Pacific Ocean, so that the **eastern** part of the state is dry and cold for good apple growing," he said.

"Eastern Washington gets eight or nine inches of rain each year. That many inches is a little more than twenty centimeters. **Western** Washington gets about 100 inches, or about 254 centimeters," Mother said.

Mr. Sanders told the children that the state is **bordered** on the north by the country of Canada, on the west by the Pacific Ocean, on the east by Idaho state, and on the south by the state of Oregon.

As they drove along, looking at the snow-capped Cascade Mountains, Mrs. Sanders said, "I'm glad everything we own is there and unloaded. We shall sleep in our home tonight. Our friends wrote that the furniture was in the house. What would we do without other people to help us?"

We all need each other, and we must remember to help others as they help us," said Mr. Sanders.

The Trip to Washington.

Fill in the blanks.

1.2   Tell what states, ocean, and country border Washington.

_____ is on the east.

_____ is on the west.

_____ is on the north.

_____ is on the south.

1.3   Washington is divided into east and west by the

_____.

SOME CITIES IN WASHINGTON

As they rode along, Joe and Debra looked at the road map. They found Indian names such as Wenatchee, the town in which they would live.

"Seattle was named for Chief Seattle," their father said. "He was a friend of early settlers." Seattle is a city in western Washington.

Walla Walla means many waters. Western Washington has many rivers and is bordered by the Pacific Ocean," said Mother.

"Tacoma means the mountain. That mountain is Mount Rainier, the highest mountain in the state," added Father.

Complete each sentence. Write the missing words in the blanks.

1.4   Seattle was named after an _____.

1.5   Walla Walla means _____.

1.6   Tacoma means _____.

1.7   The highest mountain in Washington is _____

_____.

A WELCOME-HOME PARTY FOR THE SANDERS

"Look!" said Mr. Sanders at last. "Look at your new home!"

They had driven onto a narrow road. On the hillside stood a large white house. Many trees stood around it.

Mrs. Sanders said, "Oh! I wonder if something is wrong? I see many cars in front of the house."

As they drove near to the house they saw a sign which said, "**Welcome** home to the Sanders family!"

They laughed. A party for them!

Many people came out of the house as the family stopped and got out of the car. Everybody seemed to be talking at once. The friends from church shook hands with Mr. and Mrs. Sanders. People said, "You are Debra and Joe! Welcome to Wenatchee!"

Under a tree, the table was loaded with good things to eat. The minister thanked God for the food and for bringing the Sanders family back to Washington. He asked God's blessing on them.

At last the party was over. One by one the cars left.

After everyone was gone, Debra said, "Will I ever get to know all those people? I can't remember one name now."

Debra's mother said, "I know it's hard for you now. But soon you will know the children and their families. You will like the people in the church."

"We have to thank God for these good people," said Mr. Sanders.

And that is what they did.

Complete these activities.

1.8 Write five (5) ways in which you can help new neighbors.

_____

_____

_____

_____

_____

1.9 Sometimes the letters sc have an /s/ sound as in the word science. This sound usually happens when the sc is followed by the letters e or i. Underline the words in which the sc makes the /s/ sound as in the word science.

scare   scientist   scene

scold   scissors   scary

scent   scum   scenery

1.10   The letters squ make the sound as in the word squirrel.

Circle the word that best completes each sentence. Write the word you choose on the blank.

a.   The pig will _____ if we catch it.
squeal   square   squirrel

b.   That block is _____.
squawk   squirt   square

c.   Do not _____ the tomatoes.
squint   squeeze   squeal

d.   The _____ ran up a tree.
squawk   square   squirrel

e.   The birds _____ as they fly away.
squash   squawk   square

For this Self Test, study what you have read and done. The Self Test will check what you remember.

SELF TEST 1

Write your answers in the blanks. Use the words to complete each sentence.

Columbia	Washington	Canada
Seattle	Rainier	Wenatchee
Cascade	Pacific	Idaho
Oregon		

1.01 Joe and Debra were moving to the state of

_____.

1.02 They crossed the _____ River to get to their new state.

1.03 Washington is bordered on the west by the _____ Ocean.

1.04 Joe and Debra would live in the town of

_____.

1.05 A large city is named after Chief _____.

1.06 Mount _____ is the highest mountain in the state.

1.07 The country to the north of Washington is

_____.

1.08 Washington is bordered on the east by _____.

1.09 Washington is divided into east and west by the _____ Mountains.

1.010 Washington is bordered on the south by

_____.

Tell if each sentence is true or false.

1.011 _____ Eastern Washington is hot and wet.

1.012 _____ Western Washington gets more rain than Eastern Washington.

1.013 _____ Walla Walla means the mountain.

1.014 _____ Washington has no mountains.

1.015 _____ Tacoma is an Indian name.

Match the saying with its meaning. Draw a line from the saying on the left to its meaning on the right.

1.016 "An apple a day keeps the doctor away."   That remark is silly.

1.017 "He is a rotten apple."   You spoiled my plan.

1.018 "You upset my apple cart."   Apples are good for you.

1.019 "Applesauce!"   You try to get people to be extra nice to you.

1.020 "You are an apple polisher."   He is bad.

Draw a line under the things the Sanders' new neighbors did to help them feel welcome.

1.021   They had food ready for them.

         They washed their car.

Many people came to the party.

They put up a welcome sign.

They had a party for them.

They painted the house.

They thanked God for the Sanders.

Teacher check _____

Initial   Date

20/25

EACH ANSWER, 1 POINT

My Score

II. APPLE BLOSSOM TIME

In this section you will learn about apple blossom time in Washington. You will learn how the bees help the grower get good crops. You will learn more about the state of Washington.

VOCABULARY

acre	(a cre)	A measure of land.
bandage	(band age)	Strip of cloth used to wrap a wound.
capital	(cap i tal)	Most important or leading place.

cluster	(clus ter)	A number of things of the same kind growing together.
codling moth	(cod ling moth)	A small insect that can harm apples.
elevation	(el e va tion)	How high a place is above sea level.
heal		Make well.
irrigate	(ir ri gate)	Get water to the land by using ditches.
nectar	(nec tar)	Sweet liquid found in flowers.
nursery	(nurs er y)	Place where young trees or plants are raised for sale.
pollen	(pol len)	A fine, yellow dust found inside flowers.
prune		Cut out branches that are not wanted.
temperature	(tem per a ture)	How hot or cold something is.
thorn		Sharp-pointed part on the stem or branch of a tree or plant.

SPECIAL WORD

Grand Coulee Dam

Ask your teacher to say these words with you.
Teacher check _____

Initial   Date

AN APPLE ORCHARD

Next morning Mr. and Mrs. Sanders took Debra and Joe into the orchards. Birds sang and the sun shone on the Cascade Mountains.

Debra and Joe learned more about growing apples.

As they looked at the bare trees with their hundreds of little branches, their father told them some things about apple trees.

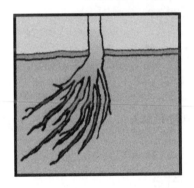 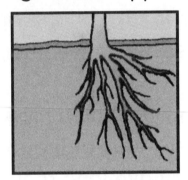 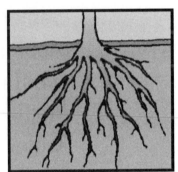

Mr. Sanders had given Debra and Joe a picture of how to plant apple trees and how not to plant them. In one of the drawings the roots were bunched together at one side of the hole. In another drawing they were spread out to one side. But in the third drawing, all of the roots were spread out in the middle. That last one where the roots were spread out in the center was the right

19 (nineteen)

way. This way of spreading the roots made them grow in all directions.

"Apple trees are short and thick. The spreading branches at the top are called the head. The bark is gray," said Mr. Sanders.

"Some things you may not have known about apples and apple growing are listed in this book on apples. I'll read a few facts to you," said Mrs. Sanders.

1. Apple trees grow best at an **elevation** of 600 feet (180 m) to 2,000 feet (600 m) above sea level.
2. Apples need cool nights in August and September to take on the right color.
3. Apples need warm weather, but not hot weather.
4. Apples grow best on a hillside so the water doesn't stay at the roots.
5. Apple trees have long roots. There should be no sand or rocks under them.
6. Apple trees should be planted in rows that are twenty feet apart.
7. The apple grower usually buys young trees in a **nursery** just as people buy rose bushes in a nursery.
8. The grower may plant as many as 108 trees to the **acre**.

9. When the trees get crowded, the grower cuts down half his trees. He then plants small, young ones in place of the old ones.

10. Older apple trees give less fruit than younger trees give.

11. Many trees live to be forty to fifty years old. One apple tree in western Washington is supposed to be 150 years old.

12. Apple wood is very hard. It is sold and used to make handles for saws.

Now Mr. Sanders had many workers in the orchard **pruning** trees. They cut off dead branches. They thinned out where branches had grown too thick. This pruning was to let growing apples have room.

Answer true **or** false.

2.1 _____ Apples are best grown on flat land.
2.2 _____ Old apple trees give less fruit.
2.3 _____ Apple wood is very soft.
2.4 _____ A grower may plant as many as 108 apple trees to an acre.
2.5 _____ Apple trees need sandy ground in which to grow.

FRUIT TREE GRAFTING

Before Debra and Joe went to school the next week they learned more about apple trees.

The apple tree is a cousin of the rosebush. Of course, bushes are not trees. And rosebushes have **thorns**, which the trees do not. Debra and Joe's father said, "Apple blossoms and rose blossoms smell almost alike. You will find that out in the spring."

Joe and Debra learned even more. The seeds from one apple tree do not always give you the same kind of apples that the seed came from. Many of these seed-grown trees give only small, sour apples. The growers have a way to make the trees give better fruit.

The grower cuts off the top of a growing tree that has strong roots. In this cut he places a strong branch that has a bud on it. Next, he fits the two pieces together and wraps them tightly like a **bandage**. It's almost like the care of a broken arm. The doctor puts the broken arm into a cast or bandages it tightly. The broken pieces grow together. God does the **healing** in your arm. He does the healing in the tree, also.

From the bud or small branch, a whole new tree grows. It grows the same kind of fruit it would have if it had not been taken from its mother tree.

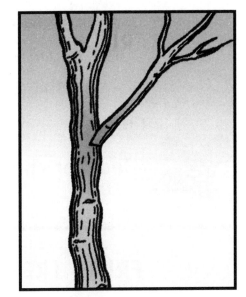

A branch is grafted.

Put the following sentences in the right order.
Write a 1 in front of what should be done first, a 2 in front of what should be done second, and so on.

2.6   _____ Place a strong branch in the cut.
         _____ Fit the two pieces together.
         _____ Cut off the top of a growing tree.
         _____ Wrap the two pieces tightly.

Complete this activity.

2.7   Write a report about the state of Washington. You will need to use an encyclopedia or other books. Write about the following things:

a. The state seal
b. How the state got its name
c. The state flag
d. The state flower

e. The state tree

f. Any other important things you find about Washington

Teacher check _____
                        Initial   Date

FRUIT TREE BLOSSOMS

It was March. Spring came. The apple trees took on a new look. Large bumps on the branches began to swell.

People began to be fruit blossom watchers. When would the first blossoms appear?

Debra and Joe learned the pink peach blossoms came out the first and second weeks in April.

Apricot blossoms were due the last week in March and the first week in April.

An Apple Blossom

24 (twenty-four)

Bartlett and winter pears came out in blossom the second and third weeks in April.

Best of all for Debra and Joe was the sight of their own apple trees turning into pink clouds. The trees blossomed the last week in April and the first weeks of May.

"God has it all planned," said their father. "The trees know when it's time to blossom." Their father told them more, "Washington is called the apple **capital** of the world because many apple trees are grown here."

Match the fruit with the time it blossoms.

2.8   Draw lines from the name of the fruit to the right time of the year.

peaches   last week in April or first weeks in May
pears   first and second weeks in April
apricots   last week in March and first week in April
apples   second and third weeks in April

FRUIT TREE POLLEN

By May, all the trees were blossoming. The air was full of sweet smells. Debra and Joe said that the blossoms smelled like roses.

The apple growers didn't want the weather to turn cold. If the **temperature** dropped to twenty-five degrees, which is below freezing, the blossoms would die. People held prayer meetings. This year the temperature did not drop.

Soon Debra and Joe saw the bees at work. The bees had a job. They were paid in the food they found. Their food was the **nectar** from the blossoms.

Down in the middle of each apple blossom was **pollen**. When the bee went down into the blossom to get nectar, pollen stuck to its feet. The bee went to another tree. It left some of its pollen there, and picked up the second tree's pollen. This mixing of the pollen of different trees was what caused the apples to form.

The grower sometimes helped the bees with their work. The men and women workers painted blossoms with hand-gathered pollen. They used small paint brushes and sometimes a special kind of gun. They went from tree to tree just as the bees do.

The grower often mixed his trees. He planted a Jonathan tree among the Golden Delicious trees. He planted a Golden Delicious among the Jonathans. The trees needed each other's pollen.

HISTORY & GEOGRAPHY

303

LIFEPAC TEST

24/30

Name _____

Date _____

Score _____

HISTORY & GEOGRAPHY 303: LIFEPAC TEST

EACH ANSWER, 1 POINT

Answer true **or** false.

1. _____ Debra and Joe moved to Washington.

2. _____ Apple trees are planted fifty feet apart.

3. _____ Apples are related to rose bushes.

4. _____ Apple trees are pruned in winter time when no leaves are on the trees.

5. _____ Growers do not cut any blossoms from the trees.

6. _____ Different kinds of apples blossom and ripen at different times.

7. _____ Bees do not help the growers.

8. _____ Many kinds of people help with harvesting apples.

9. _____ Grand Coulee Dam does not help the people of Washington.

10. _____ Apples that are small and lopsided are thrown away.

Draw a line to match the words.

11. Walla Walla   dam
12. Seattle   river
13. Grand Coulee   cut
14. Columbia   mountains
15. Canada   Big Chief
16. Cascades   many waters
17. prune   north of Washington

Name the things that happen to the apples after the pickers have taken them from the trees and they are taken to the packing plants.

18. _____
19. _____
20. _____
21. _____
22. _____
23. _____

Name seven workers who are part of the apple growing community.

24. _____
25. _____
26. _____
27. _____
28. _____
29. _____
30. _____

NOTES

Answer these questions.

2.9　　　How do bees carry pollen from one tree to another? _____

2.10　　How do the growers help the bees in their work?

_____

2.11　　What is the name of the food the bee gets from the blossom? _____

2.12　　Are all the trees in one orchard the same kind?

_____

APPLE BLOSSOM THINNING

The end of June was blossom thinning time. The grower had the workers take away one-half to two-thirds of the blossoms.

If too many apples were allowed to grow, there would not be enough food to help them grow into large fine apples. Besides, too many apples on a **cluster** would make some of them have bad shapes.

Each cluster had five blossoms. Each cluster had one "king" bud. It always opened first. It was the largest and strongest.

The grower or his helper put a spray on the side blossoms to kill them, then all the food goes into the king bud.

27 (twenty-seven)

Can you imagine doing this spraying to all the clusters of blossoms on thousands of trees?

Debra and Joe were surprised to learn that apples got much of their food from leaves. It took thirty to forty leaves to make a good apple. They could understand now why the blossom thinning is needed.

Summer was a busy time in the orchards. Debra and Joe were out of school so they could watch the work.

First, the growers had to **irrigate**. Not enough rain fell in summer to keep the trees alive. The water came from dams like the Grand Coulee Dam which was built across the Columbia River to help Eastern farmers.

The grower watched his trees every day. He had to watch out for little **codling moths**. From these moths came worms which would go into the apples and spoil them. The grower sprayed to kill the moths.

The Codling Moth

Answer these questions.

2.13   How do growers get water for trees in dry summer? _____

2.14   What is the name of the largest bud in a cluster of blossoms? _____

2.15   How many blossoms are in a cluster of apple blossoms? _____

2.16   Why does the grower thin the blossoms?

_____

2.17   Where do the apples get much of their food for growing? _____

Complete this activity.

The long /o/ vowel sound may be made in several ways. The o is often long when used before the letter l as in word told. It is often long when used before w as in the word blow. The o can also be long when used before the e in the word toe or when followed by a consonant and a silent e in the word bone.

2.18   Draw a line under each word which has a long /o/ sound.

Joe	sold	crow
rod	hope	hot
stone	cold	mop
old	rope	bold

Try this!

You can tell the number of syllables in a word by the number of vowel sounds you **hear**. This will not be the same number of vowels you **see** in a word. Some vowels are silent.

2.19　　Write the number of vowels you see and the number of vowel sounds you hear in each of the following words. Then write the number of syllables in each word. This will be the same as the number of vowel sounds you hear.

Word	Number of Vowels You See	Number of Vowels You Hear	Number of Syllables
beg			
bean			
museum			
measure			
neighborhood			
science			
refrigerator			

Study what you have read and done for this Self Test. This Self Test will check what you remember of this part and other parts you have read.

SELF TEST 2

Answer true **or** false.

2.01 _____ Apple, pear, and apricot trees blossom at different times.

2.02 _____ Bees help apple growers by spreading pollen from tree to tree.

2.03 _____ Growers thin blossoms so they will get smaller apples.

2.04 _____ The Cascade Mountains split the state of Washington in half.

2.05 _____ Canada is Washington's neighbor on the north.

2.06 _____ Walla Walla means many waters in Indian language.

2.07 _____ Irrigation is one way to get water to apple trees.

2.08 _____ Growers spray to kill rats in the trees.

Choose a word from the list below that will correctly complete the sentences.

pruners	sprayed	people	rose
codling	welcoming	king	Seattle
clusters	Grand Coulee		

2.09   Workers who thin out apple tree branches are
_____.

2.010   Growers _____ the trees to keep insects from eating the fruit.

2.011   _____ moths damage apple crops.

2.012   _____ is the name of a dam in Washington.

2.013   Apple trees belong to the _____ family.

2.014   Apple blossoms grow in _____.

2.015   The main bud of a cluster is called a _____ bud.

2.016   _____ in a community help each other with crops.

2.017   The church people gave the Sanders family a _____ party.

2.018   _____ is a city in western Washington.

Answer these questions.

2.019   Why does the grower cut away some apple blossoms?
_____

2.020   Why does eastern Washington get less rain than the west? _____

2.021   What would happen to the apple crops if the grower could not water in the summer? _____

2.022   Are apple trees green in wintertime? _____

Name three cities in Washington that have Indian names.

2.023 _____   2.025 _____

2.024 _____

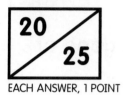

My Score

III. APPLE HARVEST TIME

In this section you will learn more about the state of Washington. You will learn how apples are **harvested** and marketed.

VOCABULARY

bin		Large box for holding things.
breathe		Draw air in and out.
bruise		Mark on the outside of a fruit caused by poor handling.
canvas	(can vas)	A strong cloth.
conveyor	(con vey or)	A moving belt that carries things from one place to another.
dairy	(dair y)	Farm where milk is produced.
festival	(fes ti val)	A special day to honor some great thing that has happened.

33 (thirty-three)

freckles	(freck les)	Small, light-brown spots on the skin.
grade		Place in order of how good or bad something is.
harvest	(har vest)	The time when crops are brought in.
juicy	(jui cy)	Runny. Full of juice.
lopsided	(lop sid ed)	Larger on one side than on the other.
prop		Hold up by placing something under or against.
spillway	(spill way)	Place for water to escape when a dam gets too full.
tray		A flat holder with a rim around it.

SPECIAL WORDS

Red Delicious   Rome Beauty
Golden Delicious   Jonathan

 Ask your teacher to say these words with you.
Teacher check _____
                                    Initial   Date

GRAND COULEE DAM IS VISITED

In July Joe and Debra went with their
Sunday school class to Grand Coulee Dam.

They went by bus. Several of the parents went with them. For miles the bus traveled along the highway near the high snow-topped Cascade Mountains.

Over the loud speaker, Mr. Jones, the driver said, "The Cascades are about the newest mountains in this part of the United States. They are not settled. Some are active volcanoes. It's as if they are not yet old enough to know to be quiet."

Everybody laughed. Mr. Jones had just asked the children to be quiet.

Mr. Jones said, "Often the land shakes and rocks fall. It has not been bad, though. Just enough to shake us up. Maybe it's good for us. It tells us that God wants us to be awake to all the good things around us.

They passed through many farming communities.

Mr. Jones talked about the Columbia River. Fishing was good in the Columbia. The fishermen caught many fish.

They passed large **dairy** farms. They stopped at a place where cheese was made. There they saw thick, white milk being turned into cheese.

They saw chicken farms.

"It takes a lot of people doing a lot of things to make up a community," said Mr. Jones.

35 (thirty-five)

"You see," said Mr. Jones, "each state of our country has something to give to the others. Just like one person has something for the other person. We share with others. It can be states or people who share."

Now they were at Grand Coulee Dam. It is one of the largest concrete dams in the United States. A large lake was behind the dam. Many boats were on the lake. The water poured over the **spillway**. The water was silvery. It made a lot of noise as it

They saw Grand Coulee Dam.

poured down. It was scary. The children remembered how much good the water did for the state.

The dam saved water for the farmers and fruit growers to use during dry times when they had no rain. Electricity was made at the dam to be used to light their houses. The dam helped stop floods in times of too much rain. Many people enjoyed the lake on their vacations.

Mr. Jones told them it took eight years to build the dam. Eight years! That was how old most of the children were!

Do these activities.

3.1   Name two kinds of farms the children saw on their trip.

_____

_____

3.2   Name the river from which many of Washington's fish are caught. _____

3.3   Name four (4) things Grand Coulee Dam does for the people of Washington.

_____

_____

_____

_____

THE APPLES RIPEN

When the children arrived back home, Debra and Joe were surprised to see how much the apples had grown. The limbs of the trees were bending over from the weight of the apples.

Mr. Sanders had many workers going through the orchards to **prop** up the branches. This was to keep them from breaking.

He gave the children a time table for when the different apples would be ripe.

From blossom time to picking time:
Jonathans take 135 days,
Red Delicious take 148 to 155 days,
Golden Delicious take 150 to 160 days, and
Winesaps and Newtons take 160 days.

The growing apples hung free. They had no other apples near them to touch them. They would have no dents in them. They would be round as they were supposed to be.

It was time for the apples to get ripe. Joe and Debra walked among the trees. They saw the Golden Delicious apples begin to turn gold with little shadings of pink. The Jonathans and the Winesaps were changing from green to a little red.

Mr. Sanders said, "Now we pray for good cool nights. Cool nights are needed for the apples to get ripe."

Mr. Adams had a pear orchard beside the Sanders' apple orchard. One day he played a joke on the children. He invited them to his house after school. He had them sit at the table. He put two bowls of fruit on the table. One was filled with apples. The other was filled with pears. How sweet the fruit smelled!

Mr. Adams said, "Debra and Joe, I want each of you to take a bite of apple, then a bite of pear." He was smiling.

He went on, "You will see how different each fruit tastes. But each is different in another way, too. God made fruit different just as He made people different."

Joe and Debra bit into their apples. The fruit was sweet and **juicy** in their mouths.

Next, they bit into the pears.

What happened? Juice splashed out of the pears. It hit their noses and ran down their chins. They laughed.

Mr. Adams explained. "The apple doesn't squirt its juice because it has tiny pockets to hold the juice. The pear doesn't have pockets, so the juice just runs when you bite into it."

Mr. Adams cut an apple into two pieces. He showed them the apple. Joe and Debra gasped. A star-like shape appeared in the middle.

The apple seeds look like a star.

Tell how many days it takes each kind of apple to go from blossom time to picking time.

3.4	Jonathans	_____
3.5	Red Delicious	_____
3.6	Golden Delicious	_____
3.7	Winesaps	_____
3.8	Newtons	_____

Answer these questions.

3.9   Why doesn't the apple squirt its juice when you bite into it? _____

_____

3.10   Why must the limbs of apple trees be propped up?

_____

_____

3.11   What does the center of an apple look like?

_____

_____

THE APPLE PICKERS ARRIVE

The apples were ready to **harvest**. The apple pickers began to arrive. They came in buses. They came in cars. They came from California. They came from New Mexico. They came from Oregon. They rented houses. They lived in house trailers. They lived in cabins. Mr. Sanders said that more than 50,000 people came to pick apples.

Many families took their vacations picking apples. They liked to be outdoors to enjoy God's world. They liked to earn extra money. Everyone was busy.

Many people pick apples.

THE APPLES ARE PICKED

Some growers had their apples picked by machines. Machines often **bruised** the fruit, or they missed apples.

Debra asked, "Can just anybody pick apples?"

Her father said, "No. You have to know how to pick them." He told her how apples are picked.

"First, you need a **canvas**-lined pail. This pail is held by wide canvas strips that cross over the picker's back.

Next, the picker doesn't just pull the apple from the tree. He holds it tightly, but carefully.

Next the picker turns the apple upward with his thumb against the stem. Then the apple snaps off into the picker's hand.

As fast as the apples are picked, they are gently put into **bins** that are scattered about the orchard. When the bins are full, they are rushed to the packing house by an orchard tractor.

The apples must always be handled carefully or they will be bruised. A bruise turns brown, and the apples will spoil. Bruised fruit will not sell."

Answer each question.

3.12 Why do you think most people come to Washington to pick apples?_____
_____

3.13 Why are machines not good for picking apples?
_____
_____

3.14 Why do you think people will not buy bruised apples? _____
_____

APPLES ARE DIFFERENT

Debra and Joe learned that you can grow more than 200 kinds of apples. But not all kinds will grow in the same place. Apples have many shapes and colors.

Apples may be round. They may be shaped like eggs. They may be **lopsided**. Some apples have **freckles.** Others do not.

Red Delicious   **Golden Delicious**   **Rome Beauty**   **Jonathan**

Some apples are small. Others are large. They may be rough. They may be smooth.

But each apple has a skin. This skin may be hard or thick.

Red Delicious, Golden Delicious, Rome Beauty, and Jonathans are just a few of the many different kinds of apples. Each kind has its own special taste. It has its own special shape. Each kind of tree blossoms at its own time, and its apples ripen at their own time.

Do this activity on another piece of paper.

3.15   Bring some apples to school. Look at the blossom end where the blossom was in springtime. Look at the stem end where it was attached to the tree. Look at the skin and color and shape of your apple. Write four sentences about it. Can you tell what kind of apple yours is by looking at the drawings of the different apples?

Teacher check _____

                   Initial   Date

APPLES ARE PACKED

When Debra and Joe went back to school in the fall, their class visited an apple-packing plant. The big bins were full of apples from the orchards.

The apples went from the bins into great tanks of water. Sometimes, Debra and Joe learned, the bins were put into big tanks of water. The apples floated out into the tanks.

Next the apples went into a washer tank. The washer tank had soap in it to wash away the dust. The apples went into another tank to take off the soap.

Next came the apple polisher. Huge roller brushes did this work. The apples came out of the polisher shining brightly.

The apples moved onto a **conveyor** belt to a sorting table. At the sorting table people who knew exactly how, sorted all the apples. They looked for well-shaped apples with no cuts, bruises, or dents in them. The most nearly perfect apples went onto one conveyor belt. The second best ones went onto another belt. The apples that were not even second best went onto still another belt. These apples were sold to be made into apple juice, applesauce, and jelly.

Do this activity.

3.16   Name three (3) foods made of apples that are not even second best.

_____

_____

_____

The best apples had to pass still more tests. They went into sizing machines. The largest and the heaviest apples were sorted from the next smaller-sized apples. The people who worked at the sizing machines had to know how to do their work. They had all done this job for a long time.

Next, the apples were packed in **trays** inside a box. It was called a "tray-pack" box. These trays keep apples from bumping and bruising each other as they are shipped.

The boxes moved on to be checked. The boxes were stamped on the outside with the **grade** of the apples. Some were marked top grade and some were marked second grade.

Debra wondered how long it took to pick, wash, grade, and pack the apples. She learned it took about twenty-four hours. The growers wanted to be sure the apples were fresh when they went to be stored in a cold place.

Write the order when each event happened.

3.17   Put the following sentences in the right order. Write a **1** in front of what happens first in the packing house, a **2** in front of what happens second, and so on.

_____ The apples go into a washer tank.
_____ The apples are polished.

_____ The apples are put in tanks of water.

_____ The apples are packed in boxes.

_____ The apples go to a rinsing tank.

_____ The apples are sorted.

_____ The apples are sized.

APPLES ARE STORED

Debra and Joe learned that apples **breathe**. It was hard to believe.

Their teacher, Miss Ray, said, "Apples don't breathe the way you do, but they have their own special way. God had a reason for having them breathe. They need fresh air inside. If the apples are left outside in open air they breathe too much and soon spoil."

"After the apples are rushed into a cold room, machines keep the room at thirty-one degrees F. Now the apples do not breathe so much. They stay fresh, crisp, and good tasting. That is why apples that are fresh can be bought in winter."

When Debra and Joe reached home from school that day they each ate an apple. The apples tasted better than any they had ever eaten. They knew so much about all the work that had brought the apple to them. They knew how many people in the community had helped to grow the apples.

Their father said, "We will soon have an apple **festival**. In our churches we have a special

Thanksgiving time for the good crops God has given us."

They thanked God for the good apple harvest.

Do this reading activity.

3.18   A suffix is a group of letters added to the end of a word. A suffix comes after the main part of the word. When the suffix -ness is added to the word sick, the word sickness is made. The suffix -teen can be added to number words. When -teen is added to the word six, the word sixteen is formed.

> sick + ness = sickness
> six + teen = sixteen

Add the suffix -ness or -teen to each of the following words to form a new word. The first one is done for you.

seven	+	teen	=	seventeen
loud	+	____	=	_____
nine	+	____	=	_____
four	+	____	=	_____
quick	+	____	=	_____
sad	+	____	=	_____

Study what you have read and done for this last Self Test. This Self Test will check what you remember in your studies of all parts in this LIFEPAC. The last Self Test will tell you what parts of the LIFEPAC you need to study again.

SELF TEST 3

Answer these questions.

3.01   What body of water is on the west side of Washington?

_____

3.02   What country is on the north of Washington?

_____

3.03   What state is on the east of Washington?

_____

3.04   What state is on the south of Washington?

_____

Name four good things Grand Coulee Dam does for the people of Washington.

3.05   _____

3.06   _____

3.07   _____

3.08   _____

Choose six workers from the list below who help with the apple crops in each community.

astronauts pruners blossom trimmers
pickers teachers washer-rinsers
sorters sailors packers
babies

3.09 _____

3.010 _____

3.011 _____

3.012 _____

3.013 _____

3.014 _____

Answer true **or** false.

3.015 _____ Apples are yanked from the trees.

3.016 _____ Different kinds of apples ripen at different times.

3.017 _____ People came from many states to pick Washington apples.

3.018 _____ If you cut an apple in two, you find a star pattern in the middle.

3.019 _____ Pears do not have pockets to hold their juice as apples do.

3.020 _____ The Cascade Mountains are restless mountains.

3.021 _____ Apples breathe.

3.022 _____ Apples go into a cold room to keep them fresh.

Name four different kinds of apples.

3.023 _____

3.024 _____

3.025 _____

3.026 _____

Match the words on the left with the words on the right by drawing a line between them.

3.027	Grand Coulee	mountains
3.028	Columbia	a city
3.029	Cascades	a river
3.030	Seattle	a dam

Teacher check _____

Initial   Date

24 / 30

EACH ANSWER, 1 POINT

My Score

Before taking the LIFEPAC Test, you should do these self checks.

1. _____ Did you do good work on your last Self Test?

2. _____ Did you study again those parts of the LIFEPAC you didn't remember?

Check one: ☐ Yes (good)

☐ No (ask your teacher)

3. _____ Do you know all the new words in "Words to Study"?

Check one: ☐ Yes (good)

☐ No (ask your teacher)

51 (fifty-one)

NOTES